WOMEN WHO WIN

Cynthia Cooper

Mia Hamm

Martina Hingis

Chamique Holdsclaw

Michelle Kwan

Lisa Leslie

Sheryl Swoopes

Venus & Serena Williams

CHELSEA HOUSE PUBLISHERS

WOMEN WHO WIN

MIA HAMM

Robert Schnakenberg

Introduction by
HANNAH STORM

CHELSEA HOUSE PUBLISHERS
Philadelphia

Frontis: *In the 1999 Women's World Cup match, Mia Hamm drives the ball down-field, displaying the speed and power that have made her a world champion.*

Produced by
21st Century Publishing and Communications, Inc.
New York, New York
http://www.21cpc.com

CHELSEA HOUSE PUBLISHERS

Editor in Chief: Stephen Reginald
Managing Editor: James D. Gallagher
Production Manager: Pamela Loos
Art Director: Sara Davis
Director of Photography: Judy L. Hasday
Senior Production Editor: J. Christopher Higgins
Publishing Coordinator: James McAvoy
Project Editor: Anne Hill

The Chelsea House World Wide Web address is
http://www.chelseahouse.com

First Printing

1 3 5 7 9 8 6 4 2

Library of Congress Cataloging-in-Publication Data

Schnakenberg, Robert.
    Mia Hamm / Robert Schnakenberg; introduction by Hannah Storm.
    p. cm. – (Women who win)
    Includes bibliographical references and index.
    Summary: Describes the life and soccer career of Mia Hamm, who helped the United States win a gold medal in soccer in the 1996 Olympics.
ISBN 0-7910-5791-7 (hc) — ISBN 0-7910-6151-5 (pbk)
1. Hamm, Mia, 1972– —Juvenile literature. 2. Soccer players—United States—Biography—Juvenile literature. 3. Women soccer players—United States—Biography—Juvenile literature. [1. Hamm, Mia, 1972– 2. Soccer players. 3. Women—Biography.] I. Title. II. Series.

GV942.7.H27 S35 2001
796.334'092—dc21
[B]   00—022840
                                                                  CIP
                                                                  AC

CONTENTS

WOMEN WHO WIN

Hannah Storm
NBC Studio Host

You go girl! Women's sports are the hottest thing going right now, with the 1900s ending in a big way. When the U.S. team won the 1999 Women's World Cup, it captured the imagination of all sports fans and served as a great inspiration for young girls everywhere to follow their dreams.

That was just the exclamation point on an explosive decade for women's sports—capped off by the Olympic gold medals for the U.S. women in hockey, softball, and basketball. All the excitement created by the U.S. national basketball team helped to launch the Women's National Basketball Association (WNBA), which began play in 1997. The fans embraced the concept, and for the first time, a successful and stable women's professional basketball league was formed.

I was the first ever play-by-play announcer for the WNBA—a big personal challenge. Broadcasting, just like sports, had some areas with limited opportunities for women. There have traditionally not been many play-by-play opportunities for women in sports television, so I had no experience. To tell you the truth, the challenge I faced was a little scary! Sometimes we are all afraid that we might not be up to a certain task. It is not easy to take risks, but unless we push ourselves we will stagnate and not grow.

Here's what happened to me. I had always wanted to do play-by-play earlier in my career, but I had never gotten the opportunity. Not that I was unhappy— I had been given studio hosting assignments that were unprecedented for a woman and my reputation was well established in the business. I was comfortable in my role . . . plus I had just had my first baby. The last thing I needed to do was suddenly tackle a new skill on national television and risk being criticized (not to mention, very stressed out!). Although I had always wanted to do play-by-play, I turned down the assignment twice, before reluctantly agreeing to give it a try. During my hosting stint of the NBA finals that year, I traveled back and forth to WNBA preseason games to practice play-by-play. I was on 11 flights in 14 days to seven different cities! My head was spinning and it was no surprise that I got sick. On the day of the first broadcast, I had to have shots just so I could go on the air without throwing up. I felt terrible and nervous, but

6

I survived my first game. I wasn't very good but gradually, week by week, I got better. By the end of the season, the TV reviews of my work were much better— *USA Today* called me "most improved."

During that 1997 season, I witnessed a lot of exciting basketball moments, from the first historic game to the first championship, won by the Houston Comets. The challenge of doing play-by-play was really exciting and I loved interviewing the women athletes and seeing the fans' enthusiasm. Over one million fans came to the games; my favorite sight was seeing young boys wearing the jerseys of female players—pretty cool. And to think I almost missed out on all of that. It reinforced the importance of taking chances and not being afraid of challenges or criticism. When we have an opportunity to follow our dreams, we need to go for it!

Thankfully, there are now more opportunities than ever for women in sports (and other areas, like broadcasting). We thank women, like those in this series, who have persevered despite lack of opportunities—women who have refused to see their limitations. Remember, women's sports has been around a long time. Way back in 396 B.C. Kyniska, a Spartan princess, won an Olympic chariot race. Of course, women weren't allowed to compete, so she was not allowed to collect her prize in person. At the 1996 Olympic games in Atlanta, Georgia, over 35,600 women competed, almost a third more than in the previous Summer Games. More than 20 new women's events have been added for the Sydney, Australia, Olympics in 2000. Women's collegiate sports continues to grow, spurred by the 1972 landmark legislation Title IX, which states that "no person in the United States shall, on the basis of sex, be excluded from participation in, be denied the benefits of, or be subjected to discrimination under any educational program or activity receiving federal financial assistance." This has set the stage for many more scholarships and opportunities for women, and now we have professional leagues as well. No longer do the most talented basketball players in the country have to go to Europe or Asia to earn a living.

The women in this series did not have as many opportunities as you have today. But they were persistent through all obstacles, both on the court and off. I can tell you that Cynthia Cooper is the strongest woman I know. What is it that makes Cynthia and the rest of the women included in this series so special? They are not afraid to share their struggles and their stories with us. Their willingness to show us their emotions, open their hearts, bare their souls, and let us into their lives is what, in my mind, separates them from their male counterparts. So accept this gift of their remarkable stories and be inspired. Because *you*, too, have what it takes to follow your dreams.

1

COMING UP ROSES

It was over—and yet it was just beginning. After 90 minutes of scoreless play and 30 minutes of sudden-death overtime, the 1999 Women's World Cup final between the United States and China was to be decided by penalty kicks. Each team got five free shots from the penalty spot until one team outscored the other. The stakes were enormous. Both squads huddled to choose their shooters.

At first, Mia Hamm did not want to make the penalty kick. She knew that these difficult shots, in which a player must go one-on-one against a goalkeeper, were one of the weaker points of her game. And with Team USA's penalty-kick specialist, Michelle Akers, already sidelined with dehydration and heat exhaustion, Mia did not want to do anything to let her teammates down. She approached assistant coach Lauren Gregg and asked her to let Shannon MacMillan make the attempt instead. No dice, said Coach Gregg. She had already penciled in Mia's name on the official card listing the penalty-kick order. Mia, Team USA's emotional leader and the greatest scorer in the history of women's soccer, would kick fourth.

Crowds pack the famed Rose Bowl in Pasadena, California. Mia Hamm did not disappoint her fans when she scored a crucial goal in the final match of the 1999 Women's World Cup and brought her team to victory.

Her stomach churning, Mia watched from the sidelines as the opposing shooters began their duel. The Rose Bowl was roaring with excitement. More than 90,000 people—the largest crowd ever to watch a women's sporting event in U.S. history—were on hand to witness the match. Mia knew that somewhere up in the sun-drenched stands, her husband, Marine Captain Christian Corey, was watching. He had been granted leave on short notice and had flown in from Japan to surprise Mia on the day of the final. It felt good to have him by her side at this historic moment. Still, Mia knew she would not feel totally at ease until her turn to kick had come and gone.

One by one, the penalty kickers drilled their shots past the helpless goalkeepers. Americans Carla Overbeck and Joy Fawcett both scored but were matched in turn by their Chinese counterparts Xie Huilin and Qiu Haiyan. On China's third kick, however, the door was opened for a U.S. victory as goalkeeper Briana Scurry punched aside a penalty kick from China's Liu Ying. Watching the failed shot roll harmlessly away from the goal, a juiced-up Scurry jumped to her feet and raised her fists in the air to ignite the crowd. Team USA had the advantage.

"I had a feeling when [Liu Ying] was walking up that I could get that one," Scurry said after the match. "I knew I just had to make one save because I knew my teammates would make their shots."

The tension mounted as Team USA's Kristine Lilly and China's Zhang Ouying both scored, making it three goals apiece. Now it was Mia's turn. If she could put her kick past the goal-keeper, her team would get a chance to kick for

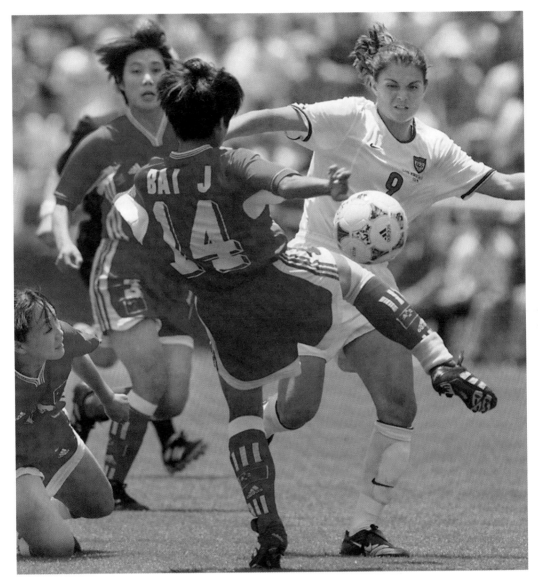

the championship on its next attempt no matter what the Chinese player did. It was a huge responsibility, but one that Mia had been preparing for her entire life.

Some observers said it had been a disappointing tournament for the soccer superstar. She had scored only two goals in three weeks of

Mia is an all-around soccer player, excelling at both defensive and offensive play. Here, she successfully blocks a kick during the 1999 Women's World Cup match against China.

President Bill Clinton (center) cheered from the stands as Team USA defeated China and later joined Mia (standing next to the president) and her jubilant teammates to celebrate their victory. California governor Gray Davis (right) also offered his congratulations to the team.

Women's World Cup play, as opposing teams had crafted game plans designed to stop her at all costs. In the last two contests, she had been bothered by a strained hamstring and did not score at all. Mia remained confident, however. She knew that soccer was about more than just scoring goals. It was about team play, good defense, and drawing penalties—all aspects of the game that she had excelled at throughout the tournament. Of course, it was also about coming through in the clutch—something Mia had proven she could do at every stage of her athletic career.

Determined, Mia approached the penalty spot, located about 12 yards from the net. China's goalkeeper, Gao Hong, stared back at her, smiling and trying to catch Mia's eye. Team

USA was well aware of Gao's strategy, however, which was to rattle her opponents' nerves. Mia remained focused on the soccer ball. Like a baseball player two strikes down with the bases loaded, she would have one chance to succeed—or else put her team in an almost impossible situation. Calmly, Mia approached the ball at a brisk run. She booted it squarely and with great force, sending a screaming shot into the corner of the goal and past a diving Gao Hong. Score! Now Team USA would have a chance to win it all.

After Chinese star Sun Wen scored on her team's fifth and final attempt, each side had four goals. Five goals meant victory—and that meant Team USA's Brandi Chastain held the Women's World Cup in her hands (or, more specifically, in the toes of her left foot). If Mia had felt nervous before *her* kick, that was nothing compared to what Brandi was feeling. She was thinking back to a match against China in March, when she had missed on a penalty-kick attempt that cost her team the victory.

"When Mia made hers, I was like, 'Oh, my God, I have the last kick,'" Chastain said later. "But that's when the calm came over [me]."

Mia and the rest of the American team stood on the sidelines as Chastain waited for the official to blow his whistle. When he did, Chastain calmly approached the ball and struck it with great power toward the upper right corner of the net. Again, Gao Hong went flying, and again she came up just inches short. The ball sailed through and the United States had won. As the fans erupted in cheers, Chastain ripped off her shirt and waved it at the crowd in triumph. Soon Mia and the rest of her teammates were leaping into a huge pile on top of Chastain. In

Eager fans crowd around Mia as she signs autographs. A role model for young athletes, especially for girls, Mia spends a great deal of time promoting soccer and other sports for young people.

the stands, Mia's husband shared a high five with the man in the seat next to him—President Bill Clinton. The stadium rang with the crowd's chant: "U.S.A.! U.S.A.!" One person held up a sign that said simply: "Girls Rule!"

For the U.S. women's team, months of hard work had paid off with international soccer's greatest championship. The win over China capped three weeks of "Women's World Cup Fever" in America. Record crowds had turned out to support Team USA, from its first contest on June 19th to its last. Millions more tuned in to follow the squad's progress on television. Some people even predicted a new boom in soccer playing for both boys and girls. In the locker room after the victory, Team USA head coach Tony DiCicco praised the players' effort.

"This is a team that just fought and fought and fought," DiCicco said. "There were so many things they had to overcome to win this tournament, most of all an outstanding China team. America should be very proud of them, they're quite a group of young ladies."

Over the next few weeks, America would learn a lot more about its Women's World Cup heroines. Mia, Brandi Chastain, Briana Scurry, and the other players celebrated with a victory tour of TV talk shows and outdoor rallies. The women received keys to a number of cities and met all sorts of famous people, including the president of the United States. Everywhere they went, they talked about the value of teamwork and the joy of playing soccer. As the team's spokesperson and leader, Mia realized more than anyone else the importance of this victory for women's soccer.

"We came to understand that this World Cup wasn't just about us making it to Pasadena and winning," she told an interviewer. "This is a historic event far beyond any single result. If we lose sight of that, everything we did would be for nothing."

2

THE GIRL'S GOT GAME

Mia's road to glory in Pasadena, California, began on playing fields far away in a much different place. Though she was born in Selma, Alabama, on March 17, 1972, Mariel Margaret Hamm spent much of her childhood in Italy, where her father, William Hamm, was stationed as a United States air force pilot.

Her mother, Stephanie Hamm, was the first to bestow Mariel's lifelong nickname on her—Mia. A professional ballerina, Stephanie Hamm had fond memories of a dance teacher called Mia. Mia grew up with three siblings, two older sisters and an older brother—an orphan whom the Hamms adopted in 1977. The family lived on the air force base in Florence, an Italian city famous as the birthplace of the Renaissance. As a toddler, Mia was surrounded by the arts, from painting to music to dance. She was also introduced at an early age to another Italian passion— soccer.

Frustrated by the lack of American sports action in Europe, Mia's father turned to watching soccer to occupy his leisure time. Before long, he was taking his entire family

Mia explains the finer points of soccer to a group of young people at a soccer clinic. Growing up, Mia developed her soccer skills by playing on boys' teams in junior leagues and in club teams, where she made an impressive showing as a teenager.

with him to various amateur and professional games. Though still a child, Mia was enraptured by the fast-paced game. At times she even tried to scamper onto the field to join the action. When she got a little older, she tried playing the game for real, joining some other children on the air force base for an impromptu "pick-up" game on the playground. The energy and exuberance young Mia showed when she chased the black-and-white ball prompted her mother to describe her as a "little ball of fire."

When Mia was four years old, her family moved back to the United States. After a brief stay in California, they eventually settled in Wichita Falls, Texas. At first, it seemed as if the love of soccer Mia had developed overseas would wither once she returned to her own country, where few organized soccer leagues existed in the late 1970s. But the Hamms were pleasantly surprised to learn there was a youth soccer program in their new community. The worldwide popularity of Pele, the great Brazilian soccer star, had generated renewed interest in the game in the United States. A new professional league, the North American Soccer League (NASL), with clubs in most major cities, had also been formed. Unfortunately, no professional women's league had yet been organized—and one would not be for many years to come.

Still fascinated by the game of soccer, Bill Hamm signed up to become a coach in the Wichita Falls Pee Wee League. At the time, Mia was still too young to join in the fun, so she spent her Saturday afternoons watching her father coach and her brother and sisters play. The "ball of fire" could not be contained, however. The four-year-old was soon chasing every loose ball and getting her kicks in.

Mia was so full of energy that her mother decided to enroll her in a ballet class to let off some steam. "I thought because she was so petite, she'd be ideal," Stephanie Hamm recalled later. There was just one problem: "[S]he hated it." Mia's dance instruction lasted only one class. She found it too slow and the ballet slippers way too uncomfortable. In the end, the dainty shoes were put away in favor of soccer cleats while Mia waited patiently for her fifth birthday and the chance to join the youth league with her brother and sisters.

Brazil's soccer champion, the great Pele, leaves the ground as he kicks the ball over his head during a game in 1968. Thanks to Pele's incredible skill, soccer gained renewed interest among Americans.

When she finally got her opportunity, Mia made the most of it. Though she was one of the smallest players on her team, she soon discovered she had a knack for putting the ball in the net. "Our team record wasn't very good," she recalled later, "but I did manage to score a lot of goals." Organized soccer also became a way for the quiet, timid Mia to overcome her shyness and make new friends. Most importantly, it was a lot more fun than dance class. At the age of five, Mia had found her life's calling.

Soccer wasn't the only game that Mia played. She also enjoyed football and basketball, and she was one of the first girls in her town to play Little League baseball. From age five, her constant companion in these playground pursuits was her older brother, Garrett. Just three years apart in age, the athletic children quickly became inseparable. Garrett introduced Mia to a lot of his friends and made sure to pick her for his team when it came time to play. She was his secret weapon. The secret didn't last too long,

Mia toes the ball down the field during a practice session. Although she is slight in figure, her amazing speed on the field allows her to fly past her opponents.

however. The older boys soon learned that a girl can be just as good as a boy when it comes to batting a ball, catching a pass, or throwing down a slam dunk.

Though she excelled at any sport she played, soccer retained a special place in Mia's heart, and in the hearts of the entire Hamm family. In 1982, they huddled around the television set to watch Mexican TV broadcasts of the World Cup. The international tournament, held once every four years, brought together teams composed of all-stars from all of the world's soccer-playing countries. What the Super Bowl is to professional football, the World Cup is to soccer. Held that year in Spain, the World Cup featured one of its most exciting finishes ever, when Italy defeated the favored West German squad 3-1 in the final game. Watching the world's best soccer players perform on the sport's greatest stage opened Mia's eyes to the game's international impor-tance. It also made her realize how much skill and determination it takes to become a really great player. During breaks in the competition, she and her brother and sisters often went out-side and imitated some of the heroes they had just seen on TV. Mia dreamed of one day com-peting on the same level as these players.

It was becoming increasingly clear that Mia *did* have a special talent that placed her far above her contemporaries. She emerged as the star of the under-10 division, catching the eye of the local high school coach, Lou Pearce. "The other players were predictable, but Mia flowed," Pearce later observed. "She was beyond her years in what she was doing." One of the reasons Mia was so good was that she never played on a girls' soccer team. Playing against boys gave the youngster an added incentive to prove she could compete on their level. "By working with the boys all the time, she developed skills beyond her years and at a higher level than the other girls," Pearce asserted.

When she was old enough, Mia started playing school sports. One of the first she tried out for was football. It never occurred to her that junior high football is an all-male sport. When she found that out, Mia became even more determined to make the team. She knew from her playground experience that she was as good as any boy in school. Luckily for her, most of the boys knew it too. Several of them spoke up for Mia to the football coach, who agreed to let her try out for the team. As usual, once she got her opportunity, Mia made the most of it. She made the squad with ease and even rose to its most important position, quarterback. With her speed and a powerful foot developed on the soccer field, however, wide receiver and kicker proved to be her best positions.

Mia might have stuck with football throughout high school if not for her size. While her male companions were experiencing their first big growth spurts, Mia remained slight in stature, unable to take the pounding that comes on the football field. Increasingly, she devoted her attention to her first love, soccer. In that sport, she found that her size was an asset, providing the extra quickness that allowed her to blow past defenders. Entering her teen years, Mia found herself growing even more dominant compared to her teammates and opponents. The opposing teams routinely sent two or three of their players to double- and triple-team Mia whenever she touched the ball. Still they could not stop her. She often seemed to be playing at a different speed than everyone else.

By the time she was 13, Mia had just about outgrown youth leagues. She did enjoy one final crowning moment, however, when she led an all-boys Wichita Falls team to the under-14 city championship. Playing inspired defense as well as her usual superb offense, Mia helped shut down the leading scorer for Iowa Park and eventually booted in the game-tying goal. "She orchestrated the team on the field," coach Lou Pearce recalled later. The tense final game lasted through two overtime periods and went through 15 penalty kickers in a shoot-out round before Wichita Falls emerged victorious.

After "graduating" from youth soccer, Mia sought out new challenges. She hooked up with a series of club teams composed of the best players in the state of Texas. One day when she was 14 years old, she traveled to Dallas to practice with one of the teams. A rainstorm forced the girls' team to cancel practice, at which point the coach suggested Mia join a scrimmage with the boys' team. Playing with a squad of 16-year-old boys, Mia was intimidated at first and did not even touch the ball in the first half. Overcoming her nervousness in the second half, however, she exploded for three goals in her team's 3-0 victory. Even the older boys had to admit that this girl had serious game.

One of the many people impressed by Mia's all-state performances was John Cossaboon, the coach of the United States women's soccer development team. Cossaboon's job was to find the best teenage players in the country and then develop their skills with an eye toward building the next U.S. Olympic team. He was immediately impressed with Mia's offensive and defensive ability, along with her leadership skills on the soccer field. He began asking people about her and was shocked to find out she was the youngest player on the field. Believing he had discovered the person to lead the next Olympic team, he asked Mia to join the development squad as soon as possible.

It was a monumental turning point in Mia's life. She was being given a chance to make soccer her full-time career and to compete on the international stage like her World Cup heroes. More importantly, she would have a chance to play alongside the best women players in the United States, an athletic education that could lead to college scholarships and—who could tell—maybe one day a chance to play in a women's professional soccer league. For a young woman with a pioneer's heart, it was too good an offer to pass up. After discussing it with her parents, Mia leapt at the chance to join the world's soccer elite. It was like the dawn of a whole new world.

3

SOCCER SCHOOL

The Olympic development team was like a school, except that it was entirely devoted to Mia's favorite game. The faculty was composed of some of the greatest coaching minds in the country, including John Cossaboon and Anson Dorrance, the head coach of the U.S. women's national soccer team and a legend in the sport. Among the students were some of the brightest lights in women's soccer, such as Michelle Akers, the dynamic kicker who many people considered the finest player in the women's game. For a freshman like Mia, however, the soccer school was a nerve-wracking place.

Mia reported to soccer school in 1986 at the age of 14. Her first day in "class" provided the bruising lesson that she was not in juniors anymore. Showing up bright and early for her first training session with the team, Mia was ready to make a good impression on her coaches and teammates. Instead of a class, however, she was subjected to the workout of her life, a grueling fitness and weight-lifting session that lasted several hours and left her completely exhausted. Mia was about ready to collapse when the

Still a teenager when she entered soccer school, Mia spent grueling hours working out to hone her natural skills and learn the strategies and discipline necessary to be a winner. The devices she rests beside here are dummy defensemen, which test a player's skill at maneuvering.

coaches called an end to the workout. But that was not all they had in store for Mia and her fellow prospective Olympians. Just when she thought her ordeal was about to end, the team was ordered to sprint outside for soccer practice. For two more hours, Mia battled muscle cramps and exhausted legs as she was prodded through a battery of drills and scrimmages. Finally, it was all over. The coaches called a halt to the practice and sent the grateful team members to the showers.

That night, a worn-out Mia looked back with satisfaction on her first day in soccer school. It had been the most tiring day of her life, but she had made it through without giving up. The experience opened her eyes to the level of dedication she would need to foster if she was to become a U.S. Olympian. No longer would she be able to slide by on her superior talent alone. Making it in soccer school would require her to work hard to remain in tip-top condition. Furthermore, a place on the team was by no means assured, as it had been on her junior teams. Now she would be competing for playing time with other girls who possessed as much talent as she did. Only those who matched their ability with a burning desire to win would succeed. The challenge to become the best made Mia think about soccer in a whole new way.

Another positive influence on Mia during her early days in soccer school was Anson Dorrance, head coach of the U.S. women's national soccer team. A former men's soccer coach at the University of North Carolina (UNC), Dorrance had been instrumental in getting the school's women's soccer program off the ground in 1979. Three years later, he led the UNC Tar Heels to

the first-ever National College Athletics Association (NCAA) women's soccer championship. It was the first of five titles he would win at UNC in the 1980s, an achievement that earned him selection as the head coach of the U.S. women's national soccer team in 1986.

As the leader of the national squad, Dorrance devoted himself to scouting out the finest talent in American women's soccer. But nothing he had seen before prepared him for the first time he watched Mia play at an under-19 tournament in New Orleans, Louisiana. Mia absolutely

Mia gets help from a trainer in a stretching exercise. She needs to be exceptionally fit to be a winning soccer player, and hours of practice and exercise as well as determination and discipline are required to be the best.

astounded even an experienced talent evaluator like Dorrance with her breakneck speed on the field. "I watched her take a seven-yard run at the ball," Dorrance later recalled. "And I said, 'Oh, my gosh!' I'd never seen speed like that in the women's game." Dorrance later compared Mia's phenomenal acceleration to a ball being shot out of a cannon. Not only was she fast, Dorrance observed, but she had an uncanny ability to blow past defenders on her way to the goal. Experience and discipline were the only attributes that Mia lacked, Dorrance concluded, and he felt sure that he could help her develop those skills as well.

Over the next few weeks, Dorrance and his coaching staff worked with Mia to refine her raw talent. Under their tutelage, she learned more about the intricate strategies of the game of soccer. Before that time, Mia later admitted, she didn't have a solid grasp of the game's fundamentals. "Tactically [tactics have to do with positioning and movement], I didn't know what to do," she said later. All she knew was how to blow past people and aim for the goal. Now she began to understand the team concept of how many different parts fit together to function as one unit.

When the Olympic development team's training camp wrapped up, Mia returned home from soccer school. Her soccer education was far from over, however. Inspired by the experience of playing alongside the best, Mia now set her sights on making the women's national team, helping her high school team win a state championship, and attending the University of North Carolina for advanced study with Coach Dorrance. The first of those goals came to fruition in the summer of 1987 when Anson

Dorrance officially added Mia to the U.S. national squad. That August, while most girls her age were enjoying their summer vacations, Mia packed her bags and departed for the People's Republic of China, where the American women were set to play two matches against the highly regarded Chinese national team.

It was the experience of a lifetime for Mia. She got her first chance to play for the U.S. national team in a game attended by thousands of excited spectators in the ancient city of Tianjin. Entering the game as a substitute, a nervous Mia concentrated mostly on her defense rather than her offense. She was determined not to do anything to hurt the team's chances. The careful approach may have deprived her of a chance to show off her explosive scoring ability, but it was just the kind of selfless play the team needed in a tightly played contest. The United States defeated China 2-0 to put a triumphant finish on Mia's first day of international competition.

After starring on the international stage, Mia now faced the prospect of returning to the everyday world of high school. The normal routine of tests, term papers, and soccer practice might have seemed like a comedown after the excitement of the summer, but new challenges awaited her back in the United States. Her father announced that he was being transferred to a base in northern Virginia. The whole family was forced to pack up and move in time for Mia to begin the 11th grade. At this point, Mia was an old pro at adapting to new surroundings and making new friends. She also looked forward to living closer to the University of North Carolina, from which she had already received a scholarship offer to play soccer.

For Mia, shown third from the right with her teammates, working toward her goal to be a champion player meant giving up much of her free time and social life. She did find time, however, to enjoy a brief moment of fun joining the others in showing how to kick a ball.

To further her college goals, Mia arranged with the administration of her new school, Lake Braddock High, to allow her to graduate a year early if she completed all her academic work during her junior term. It would put a serious crimp on her free time, but Mia was willing to put aside her social life for a year in order to live out her dream of playing soccer full-time. When she wasn't in the library studying, Mia prepped for the coming spring soccer season by playing with a local club team, the Braddock Road Shooting Stars. She was impressed by the level of competition in her new surroundings. The suburbs around Washington, D.C., Mia quickly found out, are a hotbed for girls' soccer.

In the spring of 1989, the Lake Braddock Bruins were ready to contend for the Virginia state high school soccer championship, as they had the previous two years. Of the 11 starters who had played in the championship game in 1988, eight were returning for another shot at the title. The addition of the talented Mia to the squad made the Bruins an instant favorite in the eyes of many local observers.

Mia reported to her first practice at Lake Braddock determined to make a good impression on her teammates. Many of them had already played with her on the Braddock Road Shooting Stars. For the others and for the Bruins' coach, Carolyn Rice, Mia quickly provided a lesson in her explosive scoring ability. Coach Rice, in particular, was impressed by Mia's hard work and dedication. Despite all her talent, Rice observed, Mia didn't come off with an attitude or display any sign of superiority. Instead of coasting on her ability, she constantly pushed herself to grow as a soccer player—an example Rice hoped would rub off on the other players.

Mia's good showing in practice paid off. Coach Rice named her to the starting unit, alongside two of the Bruins' best players, Collette Cunningham and Liz Pike. The dynamic threesome clicked instantly, and their chemistry propelled Lake Braddock to a very successful season. For much of the year, the Bruins were undefeated and, despite a late stumble, they easily qualified for the state tournament. There, Mia set the scoring pace, notching two goals in a semifinal win over Monacan High.

In the final match against Woodbridge, the defending state champions, Mia faced her greatest challenge yet. Woodbridge had designed its game plan to stop her from getting the ball in the open field. Throughout the entire game Mia found herself shadowed by Susan Braun, the opposition's best defender. Fourteen minutes in, the contest remained scoreless. Then Mia took matters into her own hands. She broke free from the smothering Braun for just an instant as a teammate fed her the ball, which had just been stolen from an opponent. Using the same cannonball burst of speed that had so impressed Coach Anson Dorrance, she steamed toward the Woodbridge goal. She had one defender and the goalkeeper to deal with. First, to get past the one defender, Mia began changing directions rapidly, leaving the defender stumbling in her wake. Then Mia had only to boom the ball past the goalkeeper. Shooting from just outside the penalty-kick area, she blasted a shot into the right-hand corner of the goal as the keeper flailed hopelessly to the ground. The score gave Lake Braddock a 1-0 lead and a much-needed shot of momentum.

Twenty minutes later, Mia again found herself with the ball on her foot and a clear path to the goal. This time, however, the Woodbridge defenders sent two girls to double team her and block her advance. No problem. Mia simply spotted the open player, did a series of quick stop-and-go movements to confuse the two defenders and create an opening for a pass, then fed the ball perfectly to the toes of Collette Cunningham, who scored from 12 yards out to give the Bruins a near-insurmountable 2-0 advantage. Mia later added another score of her own to seal what would become a 4-1 victory. Without her offense, or the threat of her offense, Lake Braddock would have been hard-pressed to scratch out a state championship win. But Mia's selfless pass to a teammate was the move that earned her the most admiration afterward.

Mia credited her team play to her experience at soccer school. Playing for the U.S. national team had taught her that soccer is about more than scoring goals and showing off for your family and friends. The game is about finding the open teammate, playing defense, and setting an example in practice. A few weeks after winning the state championship, Mia graduated from high school determined to take those virtues with her on the next stop in her athletic journey—the University of North Carolina.

4

NORTH CAROLINA
AND BEYOND

Having graduated from soccer school with flying colors, Mia now set off for another elite institution. The University of North Carolina (UNC) at Chapel Hill is one of America's finest public universities. UNC is also home to one of the powerhouse women's soccer teams in college athletics. The Tar Heels had won three consecutive NCAA championships going into Mia's freshman year. Even more impressive, the team had not lost a game in more than four years. Mia was excited at the prospect of playing for such a successful soccer program. At the same time, she was also anxious about proving she belonged in such prestigious company.

Fortunately, Mia did not have to deal with many of the obstacles that beset the typical college freshman. She had a lot of friends on the Tar Heel team from her days on the U.S. Olympic development squad. She also had a good working relationship with head coach Anson Dorrance, who needed no introduction to Mia's dazzling ability on the soccer field. These advantages made the transition

The Old East dormitory greeted Mia when she arrived at the University of North Carolina in 1989. In addition to attending classes, Mia endured a tough practice regimen and competed in state-wide tournaments, scoring winning goals and leading the school's team to 12 straight victories during her first season.

from high school phenom to NCAA star much easier than it otherwise might have been.

Soon after getting settled into her new surroundings, Mia began attending classes. Always intrigued by the inner workings of government, she decided to major in political science, a demanding field that required much study time. When she wasn't cramming in her dorm room, Mia was learning the intricate offenses and defenses of big-time college soccer at daily practices with her Tar Heel teammates. Given all her other commitments, she found the regimen of weight training, scrimmages, and travel a challenge. She was determined, however, to earn a place on the starting five of the next NCAA championship team.

Soccer fans had high hopes for the UNC women's squad as it entered the 1989 season. The national polls ranked the Tar Heels number one before a single game was played. Once the season began, UNC did little to put a damper on those lofty expectations. The Tar Heel women played top-flight soccer from start to finish, augmenting a stingy defense with the one-two scoring punch of Mia and fellow freshman Kristine Lilly. The team closed the regular season with 12 straight victories, outscoring its opponents by a combined score of 77-6 en route to an amazing record of 21 wins, no losses, and one tie.

In the finals of the Atlantic Coast Conference (ACC) Tournament, UNC squared off with its cross-state rivals, the North Carolina State Wolfpack. At first glance, it seemed like a mismatch. The Wolfpack's record of 13-7-2 indicated the team would be easy fodder for the deep and dynamic Tar Heel attack. But the hungry Wolfpack squad jumped at the chance to upset its "big sisters" at UNC. The team torched the Tar Heel defenses for three goals in the final contest but had no answer for the two-pronged assault of Mia and Lilly. Both freshmen contributed two goals in a wild 5-3 victory. For her heroic effort, Mia was rewarded with the tournament's Most Valuable Player honor.

The two clubs met again in the semifinals of the NCAA tournament. Again, UNC came out on top, riding goals by Mia and Lilly to a 2-0 triumph. At this point only tiny Colorado College stood between the Tar Heels and another NCAA title. Having come this far, the North Carolina women would not be denied. NCAA Player of the Year Shannon Higgins took the bows in this contest, notching the clinching goal in a 2-0 win that assured the squad's place in history. To her already impressive résumé, Mia could add a new accolade: NCAA champion.

After completing her first year of study, Mia spent the summer of 1990 playing with the U.S. national team. She scored her first goal in international play and worked hard at improving her defense for the upcoming collegiate season. When autumn rolled around again, an air of excitement awaited Mia on the Chapel Hill campus. With the graduation of Shannon Higgins, many observers now looked to Mia to assume the leadership role on the Tar Heel team. The team stumbled, however, in a late-September contest against the Huskies of the University of Connecticut (UConn), losing for the first time in 103 games. No one blamed Mia for the defeat; after all, she had scored the team's only goals in the 3-2 disappointment. But she left the field that day determined to lift her level of play even higher in order to spur her teammates on to another championship.

Almost immediately, Mia emerged as the Tar Heels' undisputed leader. Her last-second goal against a scrappy George Mason squad a week after the UConn defeat provided UNC with a much-needed inspirational lift. The other players began following Mia's example and turned in some clutch performances of their own as UNC roared back to the top of the national rankings. In the ACC tournament finals, UNC faced a stiff challenge from number three-ranked Virginia. The two teams played to a scoreless tie into the second half before Mia's thunderous corner kick found a piece of the goalmouth and broke the deadlock. She later assisted on another score that iced the 2-0 victory.

The NCAA tournament finals turned out to be sweet revenge for the Tar Heels when they defeated the UConn Huskies, the team that had ended their 103-game winning streak. The 6-0 final score did scant justice to the way in which UNC dominated play, and that was without Mia scoring a single goal. She spent the entire contest as a "decoy," drawing defenders away from teammates like Kristine Lilly. That was perfectly fine with Mia. She still finished the year leading the NCAA in scoring, with 24 goals, and was happy to aid the cause of another NCAA title.

With a second successful college season under her belt, Mia turned her focus to the first-ever Women's World Cup tournament. This round-robin, pitting the world's best national teams against one another, was a chance for the Americans to prove how far women's soccer had come since its infancy in the 1970s. To succeed, the players would have to practice and play together year-round, putting aside all their other family and school commitments. Reluctantly, Mia opted to take a leave of absence from UNC to devote herself full-time to the effort.

Training camp for the Women's World Cup began soon after New Year's Day in 1991. Three months of grueling practices were designed to forge a bond among the 16 players that would work to their advantage come autumn and the start of the tournament. The fact that almost half of the women on the squad had played for Coach Dorrance at UNC made it much easier for the team to come together and work as a unit.

For Mia, there was an added challenge: a change of position. Coach Dorrance, hoping to nurture Mia's all-around game, moved her from her customary forward spot to midfielder. In that position, she would have to play tighter defense and concentrate more on assisting her teammates rather than just scoring goals. Mia looked forward to her new assignment, believing it would make her a more complete player. She did, however, admit to being nervous about the opportunity. "I just didn't want to make a mistake," she told an interviewer.

When winter turned to spring, the American national squad headed out on the road for a series of qualifying matches leading up to the Women's World Cup games. The team started out hot, winning a series of matches in Bulgaria and Haiti. When they faced up to stiffer competition in Europe and the People's Republic of China, however, they struggled. Many observers doubted the Americans' prospects of winning the Women's World Cup in mid-November.

Despite the team's struggles, Mia felt confident going into the squad's first match against Sweden. She had adjusted quickly and easily to her new position at midfield, greatly improving her defense and learning how to use her quickness to generate offensive opportunities off of turnovers. She felt certain that she and the rest of her teammates were peaking at the right time.

A 3-2 opening-round victory over Sweden seemed to justify Mia's confidence. Still, many international soccer analysts predicted a swift fall from grace for the American "Cinderellas." But it was not to be. The star-spangled soccer stars trounced Brazil 5-0 and then followed up with shutouts of Japan and Taiwan, respectively. After these victories, only Germany stood between America and an appearance in the Women's World Cup final. In its biggest upset yet, Team USA played aggressively and kept Germany back on its heels for an easy 5-2 victory. Mia's staunch defense was widely credited with dictating the action.

In the final game against Norway, America faced its toughest hurdle by far. The deep and talented Norwegian squad had barely been scratched on its way to the title game and had defeated Team USA—not once but twice—just two months before. The Americans did benefit immensely from the support of the Chinese crowd, 65,000 strong, which had fallen in love with the spunky underdogs and cheered their every move.

The first half was a nail-biter, as the two finalists battled each other to a 1-1 tie. In the second half, the Norwegians appeared ready to take control of the contest, but time and time again Mia thwarted their best offensive efforts. Her stellar defensive stops gave a wearying U.S. squad precious time to regroup and catch its collective breath. Then, in the game's final

moments, Michelle Akers made a crucial play that turned the tide in the Americans' favor. She intercepted a Norwegian pass deep in their own end and blew by an out-of-position goalkeeper to score the go-ahead goal from just six yards out. The Chinese crowd—and the American players—erupted in celebration. But the heady U.S. women quickly regained their composure and played three more minutes of solid defense to ice their astonishing upset victory. The first Women's World Cup belonged to Team USA!

With the crowd still bellowing its delight, Mia and her teammates approached the podium to receive their gold medals. Each victorious woman was also awarded an enormous bouquet

Flanked by teammates Mia and Brandi Chastain on her right and Joy Fawcett on her left, and cheered on by the crowd, Kristine Lilly raises her arms in celebration of the team's victory in the Women's World Cup in 1999. Their first such victory in 1991, however, went virtually unnoticed by most Americans.

To honor Team USA's victory in the 1991 Women's World Cup, the Chinese hosts of the tournament put on a dazzling display of fireworks.

of flowers. Normally quiet and reserved, Coach Anson Dorrance wept and hooted with joy during the raucous celebration that followed. In the spirit of the host country, Chinese fireworks exploded into the air to mark the ceremony.

Would any of the explosions be heard back home, however? While the 1991 Women's World Cup victory was enormous news on campuses and in clubs where women's soccer was played, it was barely reported in the mainstream sports media. Most Americans did not even know there *was* a Women's World Cup, much less that their own country had won. That was all beginning to change, however. The visibility of women's soccer was about to get a huge boost in the form of rising star Mia. By the time the next Women's World Cup rolled around, in 1995, the sport was impossible to ignore. And it would take only another four-year cycle to make the tournament—and its American heroes—household names the world over.

5

TRIUMPH AND DISAPPOINTMENT

Mia returned to the leafy campus of the University of North Carolina in the fall of 1992. For a player so steeped in international glory, it could have been a come-down to resume the grind of college studies and soccer. But Mia was chomping at the bit to get back on the field and into the classroom. In her absence, UNC had added another NCAA championship to its collection. Now the school was going for an unprecedented seventh title in a row. It was an opportunity to make history, and one that was worth almost as much to Mia as the World Cup.

Much improved in her year away from the college game, Mia had finally blossomed into the all-around player Coach Dorrance always believed she could be. Mia and the returning Player of the Year Kristine Lilly formed one of the most lethal forward combinations in NCAA soccer. Mia was such a threat on defense that she could still contribute even on a day when swarming defenders succeeded in shutting her down. From the season's opening whistle, she was the undisputed dominant player in the women's game. She led the nation in both goals and assists, and the

Mia is nearly crushed by her excited teammates as they con-gratulate her on her game-winning goal. Her triumph in being a champion and winning numerous accolades led to disappoint-ment, however, when she and her team suffered a defeat in the 1995 Women's World Cup.

Tar Heels benefited from her dynamic play to the tune of a 22-0 record entering the ACC Tournament final.

Against the Blue Devils, a talented Duke University team, Mia kicked her game up yet another notch. Aware that the Blue Devil defenders were focusing on her all afternoon, she turned into an assist machine, feeding a streaking Lilly for the match's first goal a little more than 16 minutes in. Then, in the second half, after Duke had tied it up, Mia converted another steal, via Lilly and teammate Rita Tower, into a go-ahead score that rallied a sagging UNC squad. Sensing the kill, Mia helped put the game away a few minutes later when she booted another pinpoint pass onto the foot of Danielle Egan for a 3-1 clinching goal. Without scoring once, Mia had totally dominated the contest. Because it was such a showcase for her ability to work within the team concept, many observers consider this the finest game Mia ever played.

To repeat as NCAA champions, UNC still had one more hill to climb. Once again, the Duke Blue Devils stood in their way. And once again, Mia was not to be denied. After Duke sprinted out to an early 1-0 advantage, Mia went to work on the vulnerable Blue Devil defenses. She boomed a shot in from 12 yards out to tie the score at the 28-minute mark of the first half. Then, after UNC's Keri Sanchez had netted one to put the Tar Heels ahead, Mia struck again, picking off an errant Duke pass and breaking clear for a score to put her team up 3-1.

Fueled by Mia's energy, UNC went on to an amazing scoring binge that turned the game into a rout. The team ran the score up to 9-1, with Mia scoring her third goal in the second half. A perfect season had come to a fitting end. The undefeated 25-0 UNC Tar Heels had secured their seventh consecutive NCAA championship. Mia was awarded Most Valuable Player honors for the tournament.

The off-season brought even more accolades. Mia was named U.S. Soccer Female Athlete of the Year for her 92-point, 33-assist performance. She did not have time to bask in this parade of honors, however. Winter brought another training camp with the U.S. national team. Once the holiday break was over, Mia returned to the quiet life of a UNC political science major, immersing herself in her studies and waiting eagerly for the fall and another soccer season.

The fall of 1993 represented the start of the final season of Mia's collegiate career. She was determined to go out as an NCAA champion. Deep down, however, she knew it would be difficult, if not impossible, for her and her teammates to repeat their 1992 performance. Legendary championship teams often find out that repeating as champions is the most difficult challenge of all. Early on, Mia resolved to play hard and not worry about replicating the results from the previous year. This mental approach worked beautifully. Mia enjoyed another solid year, notching 26 goals and 16 assists and leading UNC to another ACC championship.

In the NCAA finals, Mia played like a woman who knew this would be her last game as a college player. A crowd of 6,000 had assembled at UNC's home stadium, Fetzer Field, to watch her farewell performance. They were not to be disappointed. The Tar Heels played inspired soccer

Mia has received many awards for her outstanding achievements during her career. Here, she is honored as "Sportswoman of the Year" by the Women's Sports Foundation. Presenting the award is the president of the foundation, Hall-of-Fame basketball star Nancy Liberman-Cline (left).

from the outset. Keri Sanchez scored barely two minutes into the contest to get the jump on an overmatched George Mason squad. At halftime, Mia's teammates had staked her to a 3-0 lead. An eighth NCAA championship seemed to be in the bag but for one bit of unfinished business. In the second half, Mia stole the ball and scored on an electrifying breakaway to ice the game at 4-0. Her last college goal elicited a chorus of "Whoomp! There it is!" from the rollicking Fetzer Field crowd. In recognition of her career achievements, Coach Anson Dorrance pulled Mia from the game to allow her to bask in the standing ovation one last time. When the final whistle sounded, UNC had a 6-0 win, an eighth straight NCAA title, and one humble, teary-eyed legend crying in the arms of her jubilant teammates.

After the victory, Mia again reaped the whirlwind of postseason awards. For the second straight year, she captured ACC and national Player of the Year honors, as well as two new honors: the Mary Garber Award for ACC Female Athlete of the Year and the Honda Broderick Cup for being the most outstanding female college athlete. When the fanfare had died down, she returned to her studies and finished up her degree. In a last interview conducted before Mia left Chapel Hill, she reflected back on her glory days at UNC. She was also eager to look ahead as well. "This is my field of dreams," she said of Fetzer Field. "I've had some wonderful years here, but I don't want to sit and look at all the trophies. I don't want to live in the past—I want to live now!"

Though an important chapter of her life was over, Mia still had plenty ahead of her. In December 1994, she married Christian Corey, a U.S. Marine whom she had begun dating in college.

The Women's World Cup was coming up again in 1995, and, perhaps most importantly, she had recently been informed that women's soccer was being added as a full medal sport at the 1996 Summer Olympics in Atlanta, Georgia. This would surely provide just the international stage for which American women soccer players had long been waiting.

World soccer fans eagerly anticipated the Women's World Cup of 1995. The successful Men's World Cup, held for the first time ever in the United States, had whet America's appetite for a game long considered a European pastime. Increased notoriety brought increased funding for women's soccer. For the first time, U.S. women were paid a salary to participate, meaning they could put aside their other concerns and devote themselves entirely to soccer. The team's stars, like Mia, found they could also now make money by endorsing sneakers and other products. Mia signed a deal with Nike to promote its footwear.

Being in the spotlight also meant heightened expectations for the American squad. Four years had passed since Team USA's stirring victory in China, and most experts still predicted an American victory in the 1995 tournament, to be held in Sweden. The first sign that events might not go quite as smoothly came when Anson Dorrance announced he was stepping down as coach to devote himself full-time to his duties at UNC. New coach Tony DiCicco faced the challenge of rallying the players for another Women's World Cup win.

For a time, Team USA seemed to have picked up right where it had left off four years earlier. After losing key player Michelle Akers to illness, the Americans reeled off a streak of nine straight wins heading into the final round of matches in June 1995. There the team appeared to stall. Mia struggled to score goals, and without her offensive contribution, the team barely held on to China in the opening round.

Then, in an important match against Denmark that could have cost Team USA a spot in the final round, goalkeeper Briana Scurry was ejected for a hand-ball violation, forcing Mia to take over guarding the goal. Despite having no experience at this crucial position, Mia held off several Danish charges, including a free kick that sailed over her head and wide of the net. In the game's final moments, she made a critical save to seal her team's 2-0 win.

After that close call, the Americans rallied,

beating Australia and Japan to earn a spot in the tournament semifinals. But Mia was still mired in a scoring drought. With Michelle Akers on the sidelines, opposing defenses pulled out all the stops to shut down Mia's offensive game. That pattern continued in the semifinal match against Norway, as the disciplined Scandinavians played bruising, physical defense en route to a 1-0 upset win. They went on to defeat Germany to capture the Women's World Cup. The Americans' four-year reign as world champions was over.

It was a bitter defeat for the proud American squad. Afterward, Mia admitted that she was exhausted. The grind of year-round play, coupled with the added pressure put on her by Michelle Akers's absence from the lineup, had sapped every ounce of energy she had. Apparently even the game of soccer's most prolific scorer had her limits. There was a lesson to be learned from the disappointment, however. Looking forward to the Olympics in 1996, Mia resolved to pace herself in future games to conserve energy for the big moment. She fully expected that the U.S. team would have a chance to play for a gold medal. As it turned out, she was right on the money.

Weary and with an ice pack on her leg, Mia and the team were not able to pull off a win in the 1995 Women's World Cup.

6

GOLDEN GIRL

Following the 1995 Women's World Cup, Mia took about a month off to relax and be with her family. She then was off to Orlando, Florida, to begin practicing with the U.S. Olympic team. Mia quickly discovered a renewed sense of determination among her teammates. After their defeat in 1995, the stars of American women's soccer vowed to reclaim their place as the world's finest team at the 1996 Summer Games in Atlanta.

In the run-up matches leading to the Olympics, Team USA learned how difficult it was going to be to meet that goal. In February, the Americans lost a heartbreaking 2-1 contest to Norway, their major rivals and a team they knew they would have to face in the Olympic tournament. Then in March, Mia suffered a close call when she sprained her knee in a game against Germany. Fortunately, she was only sidelined for a few weeks and was soon back on the field terrorizing opposition defenders. All the hardships only seemed to bring the Team USA players closer together. The loss to Norway proved to be their only defeat in the five months leading up to the Olympics. When the games

Mia's crowning achievement was leading her team to victory at the 1996 Olympics in Atlanta, Georgia. Raising their arms as they prepare to receive gold medals, the team acknowledges the cheers of 70,000 fans.

began that July, Mia and her teammates were firing on all cylinders.

The opening match was played in broiling 100-degree heat against a scrappy Danish team. But the weather conditions did nothing to slow Mia's attack that day. She scored a goal, made one assist, and kept the Danish defenders totally off balance all game as the Americans won 3-0. The dynamic performance left the Danes gaping in disbelief—and most observers predicting an American gold medal.

Two days later, however, those high expectations took a hit when Mia sprained her ankle in a game against Sweden. Her teammates hung on to win the match 2-1, but were devastated to learn that Mia would miss the next game against China because of the injury. She looked on from the sidelines as her team struggled to generate an offense against a Chinese squad that did not have to worry about defending against Mia. The contest ended in a scoreless tie, but at least the United States could advance to the medal round and a rematch with Norway.

A victory in that contest would enable Team USA to play for the gold medal. Yet coach Tony DiCicco knew his team would stand little chance without Mia in the lineup. With her sore ankle threatening to severely limit her offensive game, DiCicco had a decision to make. He chose to let Mia start, figuring that the threat she caused to opposing defenses would at least force the Norwegians to cover her. Then perhaps someone else could get free for a score. Mia agreed with that game plan and vowed to give it her best effort despite the pain she was experiencing.

Coach DiCicco's strategy worked brilliantly. Defenders swarmed to stop Mia nearly every

Replacing Anson Dorrance as Team USA's coach, Tony DiCicco (pictured here with Mia arriving at an airport) faced the challenge of prepping Mia and the team for the 1996 Olympics and the Women's World Cup in California.

time she touched the ball. On one such play, she drew a critical penalty that resulted in a penalty kick. Unable to take the shot herself, Mia deferred to her teammate Michelle Akers. Akers's booming kick tied the game, and Shannon MacMillan later won it in overtime 2-1. In one shining afternoon, Team USA had avenged its Women's World Cup defeat and positioned itself to play for the gold medal in front of its home crowd.

The atmosphere in Atlanta's Sanford Stadium that day was electric. Seventy-six thousand fans showed up to chant "USA! USA!" in unison as the proud American women took the field to face

China. The thunderous response amazed the players, who were stunned to see how far soccer had come in the 1990s. They were especially excited to see all the young girls in the crowd. It was the surest sign of all that the women's game would have a long and healthy life in years to come. Before they could fully drink in the scene, however, the Americans had to gear up to clear their final hurdle to world supremacy. The referee's whistle called them back to reality.

Perhaps it was nerves, but Team USA played tentatively in the game's opening minutes. The Chinese, who had adopted a conservative game plan in their previous contest, chose to go on the attack. But the U.S. team withstood their onslaught, and when Mia boomed a low shot on goal in the game's 19th minute, it looked like a go-ahead goal. The Chinese goalkeeper made a diving save, however, and it was up to a hustling Shannon MacMillan to rap home the rebound. Goal! The United States led one to nothing.

The Chinese women would not quit. They tied the score just before the half and appeared to have the Americans on the run. Mia's ankle injury was flaring up and she was unable to provide her customary offensive surge. In the locker room at the break, she considered taking herself out of the lineup. Her teammates would not hear of it. They knew what Mia's presence on the field meant to them, and they fully expected her to do something to contribute—even if she didn't score herself.

In the second half, Mia justified the faith of her teammates. She played like a woman possessed, drawing defenders to her like bees to honey. She was denied on several of her own shots by the talented Chinese goalkeeper. Eventually, however, she found a seam in the

defense for one of her pinpoint passes, which Tiffany Millbrett eventually converted into a goal that gave Team USA a 2-1 lead. The Americans were just 22 minutes of stone-cold defense away from their gold medal.

The defense held. Unfortunately, Mia's ankle did not. Sixty seconds from the final whistle, she was forced to leave the field when her injury finally caught up with her. She walked

Straining every muscle, Mia attempts to score for Team USA as the Chinese goalie, Gao, dives to block her shot. Despite Mia's superb plays, she was forced to leave the game when her ankle gave out.

off to a resounding ovation from the crowd. Her gutsy efforts had inspired her teammates and silenced critics who said she was nothing but a goal scorer. On this day, on the greatest of all stages, Mia had proved she was the ultimate team player.

To Mia, it seemed like the longest minute of her life, but she waited in anticipation as the seconds ticked down to the end of the game and the gold medal was Team USA's. The fans waved American flags, and the band played "The Star-Spangled Banner." When it came time to present the medals, Mia had to be helped to the podium. The heavy Olympic gold medal felt as light as a feather as an international official placed it over her head.

The 1996 Olympics proved to be a watershed moment for women's soccer—and for Mia. Soon after the victory, Mia was named one of *People* magazine's 50 Most Beautiful People. It was the first sign that the shy "military brat" was about to become her sport's first international superstar. Hoping to keep a relatively low profile, Mia tried to limit her media exposure. Still, she couldn't resist signing up to do a Gatorade commercial with one of her own sports idols, Michael Jordan. The playful ad showed the two athletes squaring off in a variety of one-on-one situations. The theme was "anything you can do, I can do better."

Mia valued her newfound role-model status. In what was a sign of the times, she agreed to serve as spokesperson for a new line of Barbie dolls—soccer Barbie. The new toy was designed to encourage young girls to take up soccer and other sports. "I can kick and throw like Mia Hamm," said the doll—and millions of girls worldwide agreed.

With Mia's endorsement, the traditional Barbie doll was transformed into "Women's World Cup Soccer Barbie." Mia promoted the doll in order to encourage girls to enter soccer and other sports.

There were rough times for Mia as well. Her brother, Garrett, died of a rare blood disease in 1997. The loss was devastating, but she got past it with the help of her family and teammates. For the most part, however, the second half of the 1990s was the best time of her life. She became the number one goal scorer in the history of women's soccer and used her celebrity status to help promote the 1999 Women's World Cup in the United States. Her activities—appearing on talk shows, making commercials, and constantly talking about the importance of girls playing sports, laid the groundwork for the national frenzy that built during the summer of that year and culminated on a sunny day in the Rose Bowl before a crowd of 90,000. Notice had been served to soccer fans in the United States and worldwide: the women had arrived, and they were ready to rule!

STATISTICS

Year	Games	Goals	Assists	Points
College				
1989	23	21	4	46
1990	22	24	19	67
1992	25	32	33	97
1993	22	26	16	68
TOTAL	92	103	72	**278**
National Team				
1987	7	0	0	0
1988	8	0	0	0
1989	1	0	0	0
1990	5	4	1	9
1991	28	10	4	24
1992	2	1	0	2
1993	16	10	4	24
1994	9	10	5	25
1995	21	19	18	56
1996	23	9	18	36
1997	16	18	6	42
1998	16	19	8	46
1999	23	16	10	42
TOTAL	175	116	74	**306**

CHRONOLOGY

1972	Born March 17 in Selma, Alabama
1972–1976	Lives in Italy
1976	Family moves back to U.S. and settles in Wichita Falls, Texas
1987	Joins U.S. national team
1988	Graduates from Lake Braddock High School
1989	Wins NCAA championship with University of North Carolina (UNC)
1990	Wins NCAA championship
1991	Wins Women's World Cup
1992	Named National Player of the Year; wins NCAA championship
1993	Named National Player of the Year; wins NCAA championship
1994	Named National Player of the Year; graduates from UNC; marries Christian Corey
1996	Wins Olympic gold medal
1999	Wins Women's World Cup; named one of *Sports Illustrated for Women*'s 100 Greatest Athletes of the Century; Women's World Cup team named Female Athletes of the Year by the Associated Press
2000	Voted Outstanding Athlete of the Year by the United States Sports Academy

FURTHER READING

Christopher, Matt. *On the Field with . . . Mia Hamm.* Boston: Little, Brown & Company, 1998.

Dougherty, Terri. *Mia Hamm.* Minneapolis, MN: Abdo Publishers, 2000.

Miller, Marla. *All-American Girls.* New York: Archway, 1999.

Rambeck, Richard. *Mia Hamm.* Plymouth, MN: Child's World, 1998 .

Rutledge, Rachel. *Mia Hamm.* Brookfield, CT: Millbrook Press, 2000.

Stewart, Mark. *Mia Hamm: Good as Gold.* New York: Children's Press, 1999.

Torres, John. *Mia Hamm.* Childs, MD: Mitchell Lane Publishers, 1999.

Webber, Chloe. *Mia Hamm Rocks.* Seattle: Welcome Rain Books, 1999.

ABOUT THE AUTHOR

ROBERT SCHNAKENBERG is an author and sports fan from New York City. He has written biographies of Scottie Pippen, Karl Malone, John Stockton, and Derek Jeter. He roots for the Yankees and Knicks.

HANNAH STORM, NBC Sports play-by-play announcer, reporter, and studio host, made her debut in 1992 at Wimbledon during the All England Tennis Championships. Shortly thereafter, she was paired with Jim Lampley to cohost the *Olympic Show* for the 1992 Olympic Games in Barcelona. Later that year, Storm was named cohost of *Notre Dame Saturday*, NBC's college football pregame show. Adding to her repertoire, Storm became a reporter for the 1994 Major League All-Star Game and the pregame host for the 1995, 1997, and 1999 World Series. Storm's success as host of *NBA Showtime* during the 1997-98 season won her the role as studio host for the inaugural season of the Women's National Basketball Association in 1998.

In 1996, Storm was selected as NBC's host for the Summer Olympics in Atlanta, and she has been named as host for both the 2000 Summer Olympics in Sydney and the 2002 Winter Olympics in Salt Lake City. Storm received a Gracie Allen Award for Outstanding Personal Achievement, which was presented by the American Women in Radio and Television Foundation (AWRTF), for her coverage of the 1999 NBA Finals and 1999 World Series. She has been married to NBC Sports broadcaster Dan Hicks since 1994. They have two daughters.

INDEX